# DAYS GONE BY

## VOLUME III

### A JOURNEY, IN SEARCH OF THE SPIRITUAL POEMS
"During the ERA of the Enslavement of the Mind"

# PAUL SIMPSON HICKMAN

**CITIOFBOOKS, INC.**
3736 Eubank NE Suite A1
Albuquerque, NM 87111-3579
*www.citiofbooks.com*
Hotline:      1 (877) 389-2759
Fax:          1 (505) 930-7244

Ordering Information:

Quantity sales. Special discounts are available on quantity purchases by corporations, associations, and others. For details, contact the publisher at the address above.

Printed in the United States of America.

ISBN-13:      Softcover      979-8-89391-477-1
              eBook          979-8-89391-478-8

Library of Congress Control Number: 2024925582

# TABLE OF CONTENTS

Front Cover *(The Holy Mountain)*

Back Cover *(The Throne of the Bishop)*

# ABOUT THE POET

Paul Simpson Hickman was born in Tullahassee, Oklahoma, a small African-American township in Northeastern Oklahoma, on January 15th, 1942. He attended elementary school at Carter G. Woodson there and Dunbar and Jerusalem in Muskogee. He graduated high school in 1960 from Manual Training High School in Muskogee.

He enlisted in the Air Force, after a brief stint in academics at Los Angeles City College. He traveled to many foreign countries, making many new friends while gaining a better understanding of the world in which we live. And solidify his belief in the Eastern Orthodox religion. Paul was instrumental in developing the first Oxford Orthodox Youth Association for the parish. His religious affiliation offered him the opportunity to meet many distinguished theological scholars from Oxford University and around the world.

During his 26 years of military service, he completed five degrees. An Associate with John Handcock of Santa Maria, California, ABA with The University of Laverne, A MPA with Golden Gate University, A EMAM with Claremont Graduate University, and an EdS with the University Peabody College of Vanderbilt.

In 1979, while living in the UK near Oxford, University, he had the distinct privilege to meet on of the distinguished scholars of the Orthodox religion. Metropolitan Kallistos Ware, a Pembroke fellow at Oxford University. Metropolitan Ware was the senior Priest at the Orthodox church and instilled in him a deeper interest in theology and philosophy. In addition, to strengthen and solidify his belief in the Eastern Orthodox Religion. Paul was instrumental in developing the first Oxford Orthodox Youth Association for the parish. His religious affiliation afforded him the opportunity to meet many distinguished theological scholars from Oxford University and around the world.

While living in Greece and because of his commitment to bridge cultural gaps, he was inducted into the American Hellenic Economic Progressive Association [AHEPA] to Greece. He was instrumental in arranging for AHEPA in Athens, Greece to host a social function for the 1984 American Olympic delegation to Greece. With the Honorable Mayor Thomas Bradley, the Mayor of Los Angeles California as well as the American Embassy officials attached to Greece and other foreign dignitaries.

After retiring from the Air Force in 1987, he obtained a position as the Coordinator of the Business Department at SouthEastern College of Greece. This proved itself to be a rewarding experience. The interacting with high officials of Greece and foreign dignitaries as well as addressing members of the American Congress Entourage allowed him to broaden his perspective of life.

Several years later, he penned a poem entitled "Spirit Eagle" and submitted it to the North American Open Poetry contest. His poem was selected for publication by the National Library of Poetry in their 1995 issue entitled "Journey of the Mind". Further "Spirit Eagle" has been selected, along with eight others for a tape release entitled "The Sound Of Poetry". His poems Days Gone By and "Respect" were selected by Hilltop Record Company for inclusion in their recording project "America" scheduled for release in 1996.

In addition, the professional photographer, Al Lewis, has included his poem "The Wedding" in his wedding photo albums of all of his clients. Further, The Golden Apple Press will publish his poem "Simple Things" in their publication entitled Little Poems-Big Thoughts to be published in December 1995. The National Library of Poetry has selected him to submit any of his poems to be published in their collection of new poems by THE BEST POETS entitled "Best Poems of 1996, the anticipated publication date was early Spring 1996.

Paul, who resides part of the year in Kifisia, Greece was a Poet Laruate for 2020 and 2021 with the Global Black Caucus. His poem "The Silence for 100 Years", penned for the remembrance of the Tulsa 'Cultural' Massacre of 1921 [this poem can be found on YouTube and recited by his daughter Irene Melina Hickman] is featured on the website of the Democrats Abroad -2021. Fortuitously, he was in Tulsa for personal reasons and could monitor the events taking place there -firsthand. On June 5th the Global African/Black Caucus in conjunction with the Global Veterans and Military Families Caucus presented a program on zoom "100 YEARS AFTER: Remembering the Tulsa Massacre by Robert Scott, Co-Chair DA Germany Veterans and Military Families Caucus.

Paul was made aware of the Tulsa Massacre of 1921 and other events in his youthful days by his esteemed teachers at the Academic Manual Training High School in Muskogee. Also, he knew that the Juneteenth commemorates the end of enslavement in Texas. And the enslaved Africans were given their freedom on June 15, 1865, almost two and a half years after the Emancipation Proclamation became law. Those enslaved in the State of Texas [approximately 250,000 Africans] were finally freed on June 19, 1865. He penned a poem, "Days In and Days Out", recited by his daughter Irene Melina Hickman on YouTube as well as for the Global Black Caucus six-hour presentation in 2021.

In 2022, his second publication of Volume I of "Days Gone By"- Collection of Spiritual, Emotional, and Social Poems was published by Dorrance Publications. While volume II of "Days Gone By" -Wait Until The Sun Comes Up" was published by CITIOFBOOKS in 2023. While Volume III of "Days Gone By- A Journey-In Search of the Spiritual - Poems" will be published by CITIOFBOOKS in 2024.

In Volume III, there will be a selection of his poems from Volume I &II that addresses these times and are spiritual in nature to share with the reader. As well as, others penned for Volume III,

# INTRODUCTION TO VOLUME III

After an illustrious Military career that spanned over 26 years rising from the enlisted ranks to retire as a Regular Major. Obtaining four college degrees from Vanderbilt, Claremont Graduate University, Golden Gate University and The University of LaVerne, respectively, in the areas of Human Development and Counseling, Executive Management, Public Administration, and Economics/Business Administration.

After his military career, he became the Associate Professor of the Business Department at SouthEastern College of Athens (SEC] in Greece spanned a period of two years as the rise of enrollments went from around 400 to 4000 students.

In 1991, he returned to the United States to enroll his daughter in college. He obtained employment with the State of Maryland as a Disable Veteran Outplacement counselor [DVOP]. It was here that he penned his 1st poem © 1995 "Spirit Eagle" with many more to follow.

In 2022, his 2nd publication of Volume I of "Days Gone By"-A Collection of Spiritual, Emotional and Social Poems- was published by Dorrance Publications. Volume II of "Days Gone By: Wait Until The Sun Comes Up"- was published in 2023 by CITIOFBOOKS. While Volume III of "Days Gone By: A Journey, In Search of the Spirituals," will be published by CITIOFBOOKS in 2024 as well.

Within Volume III, there will be a selection of his poems from Volume I & II that address these times and are spiritual to share with the readers [as well as others that were penned for Volume III].

# Preface

In the process of determining the format to use in developing the poems for Volume III, I thought to use the poems in Volume I & II to accentuate the subtitle of this Volume III as well as having penned more poems for this volume -too!

The reader will find that many of the poems penned in volumes I and II were quite spiritual in nature and will help to convey the intent of volume III's "A Journey In Search of the Spiritual -Poems". This sub-title titillates the mind to garner all that one has relative to their spiritual beliefs and behaviors.

This volume was a challenge for me to keep alert in the inner mind to recognize those events and people who were in the arena of their spirituality-including myself. In the other volumes, it was quite easy for me to capture the words and put them into print without hesitation. In this volume, the worldly events were tugging and nagging at me for my attention as I sought to extract the essence of the world events-today.

You will find the connection between volumes I, II, and III poems relevant to today's events.

@ Paul Simpson Hickman – October 1, 2024

## The Patriarch Of The Hickman/Hickmon Tribe

*Rev. Jason [or "J.C.] Hickman [b. 2/8/1887, d. 11/23/1952]*
*Father: Henry Hickman [b. 1866; d. ?)*
*Mother: Malinda Hollenquest [Rawls] Hickman Lyles [b. 1870; d. 1923]*

*Rev. Jason C. Hickman, preaching at 1ˢᵗ Baptist Church, Tullahassee, OK (ca. 1952)*

*Rev. Jason C. Hickman, son (Fentress) imitating his walk. (ca. 1951)*

# Spirit Eagles

Spirit Eagles soar, not fly.

To realms beyond the visions of man.

To heights, beyond the eye.

To distances far exceeding the dreams of man.

Only to strike, when least expected.

Found as one, not in a flock.

Spirit Eagles soar, not fly.

# TO GOD, I GIVE MY SOUL

Jubilant, proud to finally
serve my country to join the
thousands of other Negroes.

To prove to the nation that I am
worthy and more than worthy.

Make my family proud of me.
To protect them from the one
called Hitler.

I am going to war!

Lost, into a sea of black waves.
Thousands, thousands march
through the regimental grind
to fight.

As a few noble help build
us into a cohesive fighting
unit. Some with the pureness
of spirit, others dog mean,
despicable, angry for what?

Weapons often misfiring, no
ammunition, food, the last of
anything.

Straggling, we lift up our weary
buddies. To fight, to earn
respect, to regain my humanity.
to return to freedom.

Freedom, my freedom, misunderstood by many, including my own.

Huh, O'friend of mine. How come you have become closer to me than my own brother?

The noise in the distance, now is growing closer.

We huddle closer and talk about going home one day. As we sat quietly in the dark, cold wet earth. the stench sweeping across our nostrils.

How sweet it is to escape these surroundings.

As we smuggle together in the night. Forever watchful for death. With death all around us.

Dear God! How is it that my fears are not as great as the other ones? For have I resolved this war with you? I do remember the teachings about You.

For you are my Protector, my Guardian, and I am the same for my combat brothers.

Seems like living in a vacuum.
No one is here, but me. As we
move forward.

No noise, no pain as my eyes
sees the events of Him all
around me. Voices unheard,
as I rise to shield my combat
brothers.

Whose Hand is this? God pulls
me closer to Himself. Suddenly,
I sink into His Bosom.

The peace, the Quietness and
the Happiness as I look back
and down. Well done, well
done He says to me.

Now, I cannot return to my
town, my home, my family
and my love. Nor do I want
to. I will wait Here for them to
come.

# SPIRIT OF VISIONS

Emerging from a mysterious trek, the Soldiers exit the Cavern of Holiness, surrounded by the mark of Christ in the center before them.

On each side, two young men hold the Apostle high above their heads.

The messenger of God in the middle, and the old woman in a silvery decorative robe glided – stoically silent.

As the Holy Smoke rose to conquer the unholy spirits, they walked slowly into the outer world.

Preceded by three women. One dressed in a purple gown with blue soft cloth shoes.

The others wearing brown robes with a large cross on their chests, with heads held rigidly forward looking.

As she danced between them, her radiant smile filled the outer world with the Holy Spirit.

And the War began…

Invisible to the eyes of the unspiritual, betrayed into a false belief of grandeur and achievement.

Far beyond the visible opulence and power. The secret forces conduct their deeds.

As the Holy Forces battle the invisible War to us.

They Voice the warnings, as we tremble at the destruction all around us.

The tools of man probe for revelations not forth coming. To seek the enlighten with unspiritual tools is in vain.

For only a few can see the forces engaged in the Battle with the Warrior Angels. As the Saints guides Them to Victory.

In the End, the Sun shines as bright as ever.

The Stars glow with new intensity.

The Waters as crystal clear as a diamond.

The Earth as green as green, and the Air as sweet as rose petals.

Then, the Holy Warriors will rest....

# THE TWO ANGELS

Tired from another busy earthly day. I slip into another dream. Still it is strange. Its reason is befuddling to me.

As I see the four pale souls that my eyes have not seen before. Sitting near a clear grassy area surrounding a small pool of clear water.

Two with great White Wings, for they are women. the other two are men, with a simple white shroud covering their bodies.

And one of the Angels is snipping the hair of one of them, just above the ear. Not a smooth, but a jagged and uneven cut.

Slowly, the milky white area just above the ear reveal its self to me. Thinking, how ugly it looks jagged, not even straight.

The man seems quite uncomfortable by all this. Not in pain, just uneasy as the Angel tries to steady his head.

I wonder why is She doing
that... Again! the earthly souls
interrupt....

# WITH OPEN EYES

1st Encounter

As I have come to know that
The brain records everything

That the eyes sees.
Yet, we cannot fathom that.

My eyes did see the time
The time to fulfill a need.

The need to keep me there.
The time surely will lapse

And away I must go.
Like in a dream filled

With noise and crowds
Of people going to where?

And, sitting here before leaving
A place of peace and quiet.

He stood and walked around
The waiting room.

Suddenly, seeing him as a
Person to know.

Beckoning, him to come over
And he did.

She -his wife-sat across the
Room and observed.

A copy of my book of poems was
Gifted to him. And he was not

A lover of poetry. As I explained to
him -these poems were not of the old school types.

She thinking-the discussion in
Support of a change in their future living place.

## 2nd Encounter

Scaling down the steel steps to
Enter the giant carrier to take to my destination.

And out of nowhere she approached
*[another robin], "Can I help You"-Of course, Not!

She too, became a need to see
'With Open Eyes'.

Being gifted with my book of poetry
For my rude retort. She was thrilled to

Receive a signed copy from a
Stranger poet traveling to the

Same destination. In this epoch of
These times.

Hopefully, some day these two
Will find this poem in "Days Gone By"

Volume III sub title-" A Journey-In
Search of The Spiritual -Poems".

As they both were that of which
Is "A Journey-In Search of The

Spiritual". The eyes saw them,
And the brain record and processed them.

But, I did not understand-truly-this meeting
To further the journey- until now-sorry Emily.

And to, the young man from Pittsburg
Who Llives in Washington, D. C. with his wife.

Out of hundreds traveling along-only- these two came
"With Open Eyes" Me?-No, not that time!

*See Volume II of Days Gone By page 4

# A New Spirit

The minutes, hours, days, months and years passed. The blessing had not yet come.

As God, searches the earth for those Pleading and hurting for a new spirit.

With knees bent, and spirits fixed upwards Towards the sky, looking into the Kingdom of Heaven with heavy hearts.

The inner tears and emotions ripping into The soul. As man attempts to correct and give that which is not in his power.

A Spirit, to bond His Unification of the spirits.

And the Golden Winged Angel descends down from Heaven, and the Feet of God.

As the Angel's hand touches the two spirits Together – God writes in His Book.

And joy touches everywhere in the home and the years pass....

# THE WEDDING

There he stood before God,
family, relative, friends and the
world.

Knowing, his desire to enshroud
this Beautiful woman, in a web
of eternal love.

And without thought, to
enslave himself to her every wish
and desire. Standing, stoically
handsome. He watches, as she
gracefully, glides to him.

She, hidden, ruptured in a
heavenly halo, Beautiful in
both spirit and body. Finally,
the happiness long waited for.
Unfolding before her eyes, like
a dream.

As God, caresses them in His
Arms. Blending into one – for
eternity. Then, the spiritual
bond, changes into an angelic
scene of honey and flowers.

Soon, they lie in a cocoon of
love, bound by God.

Now, one forever, and the days
pass....

# THE SPIRITUAL CARETAKER

To trod down the street to the church, removing the
head gear and making

The sign of the cross as all Orthodox Laity do.
Entering the church an to seemingly Heavenly

Kingdom, hundreds of Holy Icons of the Holy
Orthodox Church surrounding every nook and

Cranny on the ceiling and encased in glass with
Silver coverings. The caretaker has kept the

Church its candle holders bright and clean full of
Oil for the Holy Service[s] to take place -be it the

Holy Liturgy, a wedding, a baptismal, or a memorial.

The candles are filled with oil in their holders. And all
Of the venerable Icons glass covering are clean and

Sanitized for the Laity and done so again the next day.
Days and days upon ends , she climbs the steps into

The doors of the church. Keeping the candle holders
glistening like pure gold.

The candles laid out in their hollers. The seats aligned
Orderly like soldiers in a formation. Tending to the Laity

As though they were students. Polishing the Icons
Frequently to remove the touches of the many lips.

Taking care to make sure all preparation for the Liturgy
Is done. As the Priest takes their places to begin the Liturgy

For this day as the chanters chant the Holy Words for
All to hear. And she stands stoically bold at the gate

Frequently opening for many in search of the spirituals
As this is her duty to God and the Holy Icons.

Darting to and from down the aisles keeping to requirements
To function smoothly.

Least be subjected to snarling low voice of the non-doers.
With her chin up and eyes down staying focused on the

Chores on demand. As we come and go she stays
Longer to reset for another spiritual celebrating day.

Not one cry or self pity gesture in serving for the church
And its Priest. While the laity sits and gives their respect

To her. As she searchers for their spiritual needs for now.
For she is my spiritual friend! --"A Journey,
In Search of the Spirituals".

# Mother's – New Spirit

And the Golden Winged Angel
descended down from Heaven,
and the Face of God.

Truly, invisible to the vision
and minds of man. But not, to
the spirit of the mother.

With a Heavenly Order, the
Angel touches the spirit of the
mother, and her womb.

The pain, as the child's spirit
rises into the Arms of the
Angel. Beyond, the kingdom
of earth.

The Angel ascends before God,
and placesthe child spirit as His
feet. God, gently lifts, the child
spirit into His Arms, close to
His Bosom.

And the Child Spirit, slowly
disappears into the Kingdom
of Heaven. As the Spirit of
God, touchesThe womb. God
lays His Hands on the mother's
Spirit, and Smiles....

# HANDS

We can see the hands of God
mending the ways of man in
His quiet, silent method.

Strange, how man does not see
this unfolding before their very
eyes.

They, simply are racing to
grasp All that they can, with
regard....

It is so simple to see, just stop
And take a breather from
earthly Endeavors, as some
have.

Knowing, that there isn't much
anyone can do. For they are
racing blindly into the traps of
man.

# AN ACTION

An action that is negative
Begets a negative response.

Sometimes, when we least
Expect the events of our actions.

Will come to challenge the giver.
A return to the old days are

Inherently an impossible dream.
The past is past and cannot be

Recaptured as we visualize it in
Our minds. The best thing is

To let it go, and forge into the
Unknown. It is a bad omen to

Seek the past for God has
Already erased it to never

Return again. In Search
Of the Spirituals.

# LITTLE- DO I KNOW OF HIM
## ~Bill Trout

Little do I know of him.
Except his kindness

Towards me. As he
Delves into giving a

Hand to so many
Without regard of

The results. Except
For the good 'Glow

Of a Spark'. As
His journey continues

With grace of Him that
Chose him to deliver unto

Others who are without
Much of man kinds holdings

HE IS ONE OF THEM
In search of the spirituals.

# Unfinished

You thought it would be done. But you didn't know
That it would be so. By the Grace of God-you start
A new journey with His Angels as your Guardians.

There you sit far away from us. Yet so close.
As you feel in your heart the fire that burns
In all of God's Chosen.

Not to worry about that what follows. His Lead
And you emerge as fresh as the clear running stream.
As strong as the native Bison. As true as the arrow.
And as gentle as the cello-piano-and the violin.

There you have it. Mr. President of the United States.
Long life-sail with the winds of change. And your walks
Moves towards the destiny to accomplish the trials and
Tribulations of life.

As you walk over the hill -you are a young person's President.
Our time has passed. As you plow the road for the years to
Come.

Time crosses your footsteps in the sand. As a gentle breeze
Erases the previous path followed by so many.

Your hand with open palm points to the sky. And
Heavens sing and the thunder roars.

Now you start....

# THE BREATH OF AN ANGEL

The Angel with Great Black
Wings sweeps over the dusty
earth.

Churning up dust into Holy
Golden Flakes.

And they flow into the nostrils
of the spiritual.

Filled with a Heavenly Breath,
past the spirits. Reaching
the souls, beyond the hollow
bodies.

Lying prone on their backs,
looking upwards to the sky.
Covered with Peace and
Serenity their eyes slowly
closes....

# THE GATES

Come in! Come in! to my
small simple life. Why do you
hesitate? Are you afraid of me?

I have no power to do you harm.
I have no strength to fight you.
I have no will to combat you.
And I have no food to give you.

What makes you afraid of me?
What do you see in me that
reeks fear in your heart? I am
quiet, simple and weak. I have
very little to offer.

I merely live behind the Gates.
And I sense They are slowly
closing.

People pass me by with little
care or interest. I beckon for
you to enter into my world, if
you dare.

Are you afraid of me? I have no
power to harm you. I have no
strength to fight you. I have no
will to combat you. And I have
no food to give you.

For behind the Gates lies all
that you could want or need.

And I sense they are slowly
closing.

I left a little crack for you to
slip through – if you dare.
Hurry! Hurry! My Gates are
closing....

# IN SEARCH OF THE SPRITUALS

As the Africanoi Priest
Line up to dish out food

To the laity in the land
Of our ancestors.

The Breath of God blows
Upon them, the strength

And desire to do that
Which he ask of them.

In these times of man
Searching for the golden

Coin by any means available.
While some search for spirituality

Guidance and strength,
A peer into the Africanoi

Spiritual land are the
Remnants of the manifestation

Of western ways as there
Is a touch of the old world

Ways."The events that
Deeds that we do lead to

Our spirituals tried to
Our character. That

"Glowing Spark" leading to
The spirituals behavior likeness.

# JUST, A DIAMOND IN THE CORNER

Just, a little glitter tucked away
in a space where none may
never look.

As I peer out to see those
coming and going. And to hear
all of their secrets.

Of course, I am not that
big. That is to command the
attention of the world, or even
the acknowledgement of the
least of them.

Somehow, I am very well put
together, and am perfect in
almost every sense.

But, I am still without the
understanding of the enmity of
my existence.

I am just a diamond in the
corner - the church.

# WINDS OF THE SPIRIT

Winds of the Spirit, seeking
tocapture, the evasive souls of
life.

Silently moving, through
the realms of the universe,
unknown to many.

Gently, caressing the spirits of
those it seeks, in a cocoon of
love.

Lifting, them far above the
bonds of earth, forever into the
Mansion.

Winds of the Spirit, seeking to
capture the evasive souls of life.

# THE READER

Little as she was
Coming from a distant land.

To live with others to
conquer the bounds of another

life style. Confronted with physical
And mental challenges.

She forged ahead unrelenting
to find her place in a new world.

With graceful eyes, she watched others
move towards conquering the demands

Of some growing stronger physically
And mentally.

She dove into her hearts desire with
a soft squeaky tone-at first.

Then, builds her tone's into one '
of 'In Search for Spirituals'.

Finally, an accomplished reader of the Holy
Scriptures and A chanter of the liturgical hymn.

Completing, part of her search for the
spirituality of her life....

As I listen to her determination to stand
in the realm of being one of them.

In the years to come, I wonder
Where she will be?

And where she will go to
Complete 'the Search of the Spirituals'.

## TALK, WITH AN ANGEL

Be aware, the touch of the Spirit.
Peace, wisdom and patience.

An invitation to ride with an
Angel.

A searching by the Spirit,
known by a warm soothing
touch

Hear the message, the feeling,
the Emotion.

Life's and unbearable reality,
tomorrow    bgloomy,    hope
untouchable, days foggy.

A period of earthly troubles
Ride with your Angel.

# FROM HERE, TO THERE

Believe that God would leave,
destiny to man.

Permit man to exploit,
manipulate, and corrupt the
fruits of earth.

Be allowed, to harvest further
decadence, through endless
trials and tribulations.

Only to arrive at the same
place, a different time, from
whence man came.

Believe that God, would leave
destiny to man!

Not now, not never.

# A TALK, WITH GOD

A talk with God, tears streaming
down my face.

Emotions, and turbulence,
beyond the mind, the universe
– to Heaven.

Pain, for the plight of a people.
Ambling, with heads held
lowly. Despair, upon faces.

The world thundering pass.
God, does not see these things.

Their unheard pleas and empty
dreams. A future, too distant
and unclaimable.

They, not forgotten! A talk with
God.

# HIDDEN, NOT HIDDEN

This journey is a short distance.
To unchartered grounds-by me.

Nestled in the mist, open -yet
Hidden in an area-it sits.

Surrounded by the pine trees
Reaching for the sky.

With the black places to sit
Scattered hither and thither.

The solid rock group plattered
With white paint as the soil

Of the earth sits in the creavis
Of the Rocks.

The small church sits nestled
Among them all.

Quietly and patiently waiting for
the visitors to bring forth their

Tears and questions for resolution
of earthly pain.

As the Priest sits tucked in the small
quaint house....

# A Christmas With A Soul

Now, mortal soul
Deeply soiled.

My pride nothing royal
The pain and scars

Had for many years
Not really talked

To God, because of
Manly tears,

To stand and watch
While others play

With glee
Dancing or talking

About the Christmas
Tree.

Is this what
I want?

I need to know
To see the snow

With its pure
Clean glow

Or a Christmas with
A soul to seek and find.

Hold it tight
Because God made

It mine. Can this be
What I wish to hold?

Do I dare to be
That bold?

For Got to reach
Into my spirit

And pull out
My soul.

To gently wash and
Make whole.

Is this my
Final goal?

A Christmas with
A Soul?

# THE ANGELS SEEN IN THE MIND'S EYES.

Alexander's two Angels-
1st Angel

One just above
Your shoulders

Dark complexion
With a curly

Beard and hair
Growing out of

Control. Large
Deep black eyes

With a piercing look.
He is your guide in
Strength of character.

## 2nd Angel

Fair complexioned
With blue

Eyes and auburn hair.
His complexion is bronze

With a soft smile.
He is your guide to
Meet your aspirations.

## Irene's Three Angels

One behind you
And two by

Your side. One is
Holding your hand,

The other stands
Next to you and

One is behind you.
The one behind

You is very dark
Complexioned with very

Black eyes. Straight
Hair covered By

A white scarf and
A beige gown.

She protect you
From people who try

To pull you down
From behind.

The 2nd one is
Holding your hand

Is olive complexion
With soft brown eyes.

Dress with a light
Green scarf and

Medium green gown,
Brown sandals

With straps. Her
Hair is sort of light

Brown. She is your
Best friend.

She loves you and
Is always with you.

She is your sweetness
And character maintainer.

The 3rd one is a fighter.
She guards with vigor.

She has jet black hair
A very white complexion

With deep green eyes.
She is dressed

In a white gown
And white scarf

With sandals and
Brown straps.

She protects you
From your enemies.

# AND, SHE SENT ME A MESSAGE

As I quest to visit another
African country She boldly

Sent me a document about
The Congo- the most inter

Central country in Africa
With the history of the most

Vile behavior from one culture
Upon another. As the children

Play and move about their
Worshiping services.

While we sit in the soils
Of the past deeds of some.

As we start to suffer the
Consequences of past deeds.

They play gaily among the
Natural surroundings in

Peace and quiet. Listening and
Participating in the Holy rituals

Of the Orthodox Church with
Reverence and obedience.

Suddenly, her soul touches me
From a distance so far away.

Thanks to her sharing this
Information with me.

As I strive to capture the feeling
In -'A Journey, In Search of The

Spirituals'. Another one comes
Reminding me that the beauty

And Spirituals of Africa were
given
To us by God to Protect.

# SITTING, JUST TO LISTEN

Sitting in the warmth
Of the small room used

By men to sweat a bit.
Quietly, sitting on the

Bench in a silent mood.
As he sat bent over in a

Meditative manner. Then
Spoke that his ex-wife

Was dying and he had
No further love for her.

Listening, without the
Utterance of a word.

He covered most of his
Loss of respect for her.

After 23 years of marriage,
Due to her excessive drinking

And smoking. Now she lies
On her bed waiting for the

"Dancing Towards The Angels".
He is searching for the spirituals,

Listening without the utterance
Of one word.

As he leaves with the departing
Words " Have a good day" and

Sitting, still speechless
Thinking, these days some
Are searching for the Spirituals

# MOTHER'S – NEW SPIRIT

And the Golden Winged Angel
descended down from Heaven,
and the Face of God.

Truly, invisible to the vision
and minds of man. But not, to
the spirit of the mother.

With a Heavenly Order, the
Angel touches the spirit of the
mother, and her womb.

The pain, as the child's spirit
rises into the Arms of the
Angel. Beyond, the kingdom
of earth.

The Angel ascends before God,
and places the child spirit as
His feet. God, gently lifts, the
child spirit into His Arms,
close to His Bosom.

And the Child Spirit, slowly
disappears into the Kingdom
of Heaven. As the Spirit of
God, touches The womb. God
lays His Hands on the mother's
Spirit, and Smiles....

# CROSSING THE BRIDGE

Let's see who will cross
The bridge – What bridge?

There, to cross the bridge
Of righteousness and truth.

Versus ill behavior and lies.
Let's see who will cross the
bridge.

A Journey, In Search of the
Spirituals.

# LOST CHILD

Lord God, this mother lost a child
To You.

Hold and protect him for her.

Reasons unknown to her, unknown
to us.

What is lost will be replaced in
another way....

Appearance is not, what the eyes
see. Be not lonely, nor question.

Search for the Spirit, and touch
the work of God. Look for it, see
it, believe it.

The answer lies not from the tongues
of man, but from the Spirits of God.

And the Angels still sing to you....

# WINDS OF THE SPIRIT

Winds of the Spirit, seeking to
capture, the evasive souls of life.

Silently moving, through the realms
of the universe, unknown to many.

Gently, caressing the spirits of
those it seeks, in a cocoon of love.

Lifting, them far above the bonds of
earth, forever into the Mansion.

Winds of the Spirit, seeking to capture
the evasive souls of life.

# A Glance Or That Glance -On The Plane

If I can only stay
Out of the way of others.

To not be disturbed,
Disturbed by their

Wayward ways. To
Not lose focus for

The chore needing my
Attention. To skip away

From the distractions or
Pursuits of wealth.

To only lose their
Own selves in the

Pursuit of stuff.
Being targeted to

Receive the gift of the
Wealthy of material stuff.

Only to be stricken
Out of the ranks that

Took all of it.
As prayer to God

For not allowing the
Reap of material wealth

In place of wealth
Not of this world

In its place. To move
About unrestricted among

Those claimants of
Material wealth. While

lavishing in Spiritual Wealth.
What a gleeful and quietness.

There, my strolling where
No one knows me.

# LIFE

As the tears flow freely down her face. as the tears flow freely down their faces.

Knowing that which is about to come. The hour still unknown. Believing, those left behind will understand.

To make them enjoy the shortness of existance. As they gazed about searching, events, the time.

Not fearful of the journey into the unknown, but still afraid of the elevation.

As they stand around, being helpless. For the events, to come is not of this mortal world.

Reflecting on the chores of the years. Making amends, as time moves on swiftly.

Sleepless nights, of traveling from one world to the next.

To endure the pain of expired life, As the tears rolled down their faces.

And we stood by helpless, As
death slowly takes  them to the
Kingdom World.

# WINGS OF ANGELS

On the Wing's of Angels. Taken
From the bosom of father.

To far lands and unhallowed
Worlds. Far from the dream.

Far from the Wing's of Angels.
Through the annals of man's
Wickedness, hatred, fears.

The abyss of earthly dwellers.
To unheard heights, insight,
Respect, dignity and truth.

Soon! Heaven, Peace, Tranquility,
Happiness.

# GENTLE, THE LAMB

Gentle the lamb, peaceful
Quiet, serenity beyond belief.

A miraculous birth, the touch
of ethereality.

Unknown to man, unknown to self,
known to me.

Destiny far beyond time, strengths
infallible.

Gentle the Lamb, to the world –
to me.

# A DREAM – UNKNOWN

Walking through the narrow
street. Coming upon an old
house. And, going went inside
to explain.

Why not to visit an old friend
too long.   For having three
envelopes to deliver to a place
unknown.

Clutching      them      tightly.
Leaving in a hurried way.

Exiting the house and turned
to The left, there was an old
man. The   women's   father!
Connected to

An apparatus to his head. His
head with a large piece missing
Had  a  bald  shiny  pulsating
apparatus.

As she explained this was a new
way To prolong his life. Still
leaving hurriedly through the
street.

Probably,  being  chased  by
someone. Suddenly being lead
by a young boy.

Approaching an old building,
entering with The intent to
exiting out the back door.

The back door, it was covered
with a hanging burlap-type
cloth.

The young boy went through,
hesitating He beckoned me to
hurry through.

Near the burlap cloth was a
Nun sitting And weaving, and
a priest, and a man,

And a woman taking Holy
Communion. Apologizing for
the intrusion and the Nun

Said go ahead and pass. Still
clutching the Three envelopes
and exiting the room.

Upon reaching the outside, my
tears started Flowing like water.

Knowing, we had passed
through a blessed room. And
continued the journey to where
is

Still unknown. Clutching the
three brown old envelopes....

# A GLIMPSE OF LIFE - FOUR VIEWS

*REMEMBERING WHEN*

When we were kids and walking
down The street at night in our
neighborhoods.

Our biggest fear was the loose dogs.
And today it is the loose humans of all
Cultures.

*OUR FATHERS - THE AFRICANOI\**

To our fathers as the vain deed doers
Filled with the venom of the evil ones

Touched upon your sacred body and
Trampled it into dust from whence it

Came. As you move to your cross to
bear The sting of barbaric actions.

Your martyrdom will be inherited by
your Seeds planted for the growth of
your soul

Into the face of them. Sting their
faces and Rupturing their hearts as
their seeds their

Tied to the evil one to reap that which
was Sowed by their fathers.

"Wait Until The Sun Comes Up"!

*THE SPIRITS OF THE ANCESTORS LIVES ON*

Having heard the stories only little short stories Of the life under the yoke of other men's will.

Listened to our moms and dads reminiscing About their youthful days. Days that can only

Go back a few decades then drops off into that Unknown hollow period of " Lost Ancestors" of

The Africanoi life. Buried beneath the cover revealing The souls of the Ancient Africanoi carried from the lands.

To a strange place of iniquity. Protect us not as your Ancestors did for you, but what you must do for us.

For being cheated out of the inheritance, broken like Wild horses and domesticated into the dreams of others.

## *WHERE DO WE GO FROM HERE*

Over the mountains and across he
seas? To another land to start anew
as we bury

The soil of this ravaged one from
shore To shore, from the hills, to the
mountains....

# What Can We Say
## (To the sauna pals – Corey & Michael)

Never thought, to see them as persons to know.
Life moves swiftly, as we grasp to touch a life

Giving candle's flame. Are these times, just a
Reminiscence of the past? The stories from

Yesteryear's? With a slightly different take
But the stories, we have heard before?

Still, making gains on the knowledge of life's
Unfurling demands. As we stumble. Under

The weight of the trials of living coping with
The times, stretching out to capture its essence.

Still growing, demanding self, to stretch further
And further into the realms of the unknown.

Giving praise to God for His Wisdom in Guidance.
Protecting us. Is it really unknown? Or just a fear.

Of the future's demands, It's impact on the world,
As we see it.

# **To Steal My Life For A Day – 2003

Remember, walking down the warehouse aisles
To the abrupt

Stomp of my toe. Thinking that never happened
To me before. As I was a former jogger and ate

The proper foods. Now, my mind seems to not be
Able to solve the simplest logistical issue or

Anticipate probable supply chain delays. What gives?
Traveling, the 9 hours to my new job location on

Weekends a distance far from those dear to my heart.
As her face seemed troubled to me. As wondering why?

The blinking dashboard lights as the journey ends.
And in the early morning to awake with a splitting

Headache. Surmising that this is a serious condition.
Stumbling about to locate the phone, requesting the

Front desk to contact 911. fading in and out and
Decided to take the emergency trip to the nearest

Medical facility via helicopter fading in and out.
Giving the information needed to effect

The surgery and closing my eyes to rest. There comes
A screeching voice cracking through my peaceful

The surgery and closing my eyes to rest. There comes
A screeching voice cracking through my peaceful

Rest and thoughts [what a peaceful place to be -no noise,
No Challenges, but one regret-never finished my book of

Poetry-as This will be my eternal dream]? Waking up by
My daughter screeching voice " Daddy,! Daddy! Don't leave

Me like this-she was over 900+ miles away. Glancing about,
Realizing the form brick layered walls and lying deep in the

Bottom. The daughter reached to bring me up-to no avail.
Then, the wife-to no avail. Then a strong tanned hand and

Arm covered by a light tan sleeve, reached down and pulled
Me out of my grave. Perplexed, I asked" Why did you do that?

And who are you? "He answered, I am Saint Nicholas-
The New One"! Having been in a coma for 14 days, my

Eyes opened to see my brother and a friend sitting near
My bed. As I expressed to them "Why are you here-there

Was Nothing you could have done"! Then, the days
Afterwards to this day that was almost 20 years ago.

# WITHIN ME LIES A DREAM STORY

Do you want me to tell it to you?
Will you listen? Probably not?

Well. let me say this. Once upon
A time... Ham or Cush.

While on the que to take Holy
Communion having a choice to

Go the priest on the left
Or the right. But, there

Stood an unknown Monk [to me]
In the center. So deciding to

Go to him. Approaching to
Utter my name.

He asked of me – first! "Paul!
Which one convinced you to

Become an Orthodox to marry
Maria – Anna? Ham or Cush?"

I said Cush – reluctantly.
*AS THE DREAM ENDED HERE*

In researching the names
Of Ham and Cush learning

That Ham was the son of Noah and
Cush was the son of Ham.

In the Old Testament there
In the information.

Reading that the Cushites were
A dark skinned people.

Whose King possessed thousands
And thousands

Of men with 300 chariots…
Asa asked God to help him

Fight against the Cushites.
The Cushites were defeated

And their Kingdom destroyed.
The Cushites/Ethiopians lived

South of Egypt. And moved around
Many areas…

*As this a dream in answering my concern about the validity of the documentary of Cleopatra III. Then I researched the origin of "Cush" on the line.*

# DANCING TOWARDS THE ANGELS

And having loved so many
Of you. Some more than others.

But loved just the same.
Some went too soon as they

Were Dancing Towards the
Angels. Whirling around us,

The left behind to live without
Them to touch and hold.

As they were Dancing towards
The Angels. Some waiting, their

Turn to Dance Towards The Angels,
And yet some will not get the thrill

Of whirling through the Heavenly
Skies. Wondering, when the day comes

For their arrival to take them to the
Dance Towards The Angels.

With so many thunderous interruptions
All around making the "Dance" so strenuous

For the spirit. Encountering, obstacles to Battle thrown from so many sources,

Catching many off guard. With God's
Desire for Patient, Wisdom and Obedience,

As this will be the last of the dancing.
Being summoned to the furthermost point

In the Holy House in the mist of the
Glorifying the Water.

Hearing the young lady's chanting voice
That has grown far from a child's voice into

A solid strong spirited, gifted one.
Her chanting tones are pure and

Clear as a canary's songs. Trekking!
On the paths laid out before them a

Journey towards the Dancing…
Arriving! at the next epoch for

"Dancing Towards the Angels."

# THE DAYS TO COME

As we stand here in the dawn
Of the iniquity of man.

Solemn towards the passing
Of the glow of sunlight.

Kissing the waves of the seas
And garnering substance

From the mountains, as we
stand here.

As the trees bend and sway
With the winds of change.

As the thunder roars, and the
Lightning cracks noisily in

The cloud sky. The Days To
Come. As we stand here.

Immersed in the ways of man
That leads to nowhere for so

Many. As we wait for others
to lead us to where?

Grand parents are gone. Parents
Are gone.

As we stand here waiting for
The Days To Come…

# I AM WOKE

As I stand among you

Some must feel uncomfortable
To you. Staying in homeostasis

Is detrimental to the common
Good for all. As I am standing

Among you. As I see what you
Cannot see as I can do that

Which you cannot do.
As I live where others cannot

Live. Who are you. Where did
You come from Where did the

Winds of change pick you up
From. A mixture of cultures

From around the world. The
Beauty of the true owners

How magnificent you appear
To all of us. Having waited for

Centuries, just to take a seat
Among the conquerors

Of the hallow lands. Standing,
Here I can see you, but

Others cannot see me.
Why is that so.

Ever wonder, why is it so?
I am standing here. I AM WOKE!

# THE SPIRITUALITY OF A MOTHER

As she glides to the pew|
And sits with him next to her.

It is in pew row number seven
The pew row that his grandfather.

Sat-a spiritual friend of mine.
As she gently quiets him.

Yet, she gently keeps him close to
Her as they stroll up

For the Holy Sacrament. He twists and turns a little
As she gently holds his head forward, and he opens his mouth.

As they trod back to the pew number seven
To sit. And he has the broadest smile on his

Face of an achievement. Now, they continue
"The Journey, In Search of the Spirituals".

And this goes on for years and years.
And she keeps her gentle touch on him.

As he is removed to a better place to assist him
To develop into a better position in life.

As she flies back and forth. As he grows more
in talent and in behavioral aspects each time
he comes to spend time with us.

He is much wiser and talented. As he knows
The names of so many and even their ages.

The Priest invites him to partake in the Holy
Liturgy as one of the Alter Boys.

If he makes a misstep- looks at her- and she
Nods approval and he smiles.

And, I had a thought of wondering what does
he see in his mind that we cannot see?

As I observe this bonding relationship between a
mother and her gifted son.

Who was challenged by the intake of a
Medication that went all wrong for him.

Still, she has stood by for years as a mother
To nurture her son.

Being curious, one day- I asked "How do
You manage to maintain your gentle motherly love

And patience with him?" She replied, it is
Because of Orthodoxy that I have gained the

Strength and patience to continue my motherly
duty. As she continues "The Journey, In Search

Of the Spirituals". And, I keep watching this
beautiful spiritual mother's guidance and love
For her son.

And the 2nd son makes the journey to the Holy
Mountain. Upon his return, he steps into the partking
Of the Holy Liturgical Chants.

As this unfolds in front of our very eyes for some to see –
While many do not experience this event as I have of.
" A Journey, In Search of the Spirituals".

*THESE ARE THE FOUR PAINTINGS PAINTED BY Louis Charles Gaither – 1993 in Prince Charles County, Maryland USA.*

*The inspiration of this poem in this book entitled "LOST TALENT".*

# *Lost Talent

As he sat down with a look of hunger
in his eyes. As I searched, nothing not

Even the lowest. Sensing, a strange and
Different personality from the others.

He glanced up with a gleam in his eyes.
Within minutes, my face was on the white

Paper napkin. Just as quickly as he came
He disappeared for a long, long time.

Thinking, over the months, a talent, this
homeless and hungry person. Drifting, in

A world too busy to care. As my emotions
rose to meet my thoughts.

As quickly as he disappeared, he returned.
Looking deeply hurt in the eyes, My soul

Ripped with sorrow and anger. For I, too,
was with little. As I watched him sipping

Coffee. Knowing the thoughts of his mind
As though they were my own. The world

Would not know his talents. As I gave him
My last. Thinking, his need more important

Than mine. As I walked away. Poured down
The drain, into the sewer, into the sea.

Lost forever! As the tears, began to seep into my
Eyes. I must, I must.

*Subsequently, I provided the funds for him to purchase art supplies and agreed to purchase all of his paintings. Displayed on the previous page four (4) of them.*

## THE CELEBRATION OF THEIR 50ᵀᴴ WEDDING ANNIVERSARY

### Henry [Jim] Hickman

My father,

A man who never smoked or drank the brown whiskey. Brilliant with the number, a strong, but gentle soul who gave to the neighborhood young boys funds to keep them out of trouble.

Planted and managed several "truck patches" [gardens] and permitted shopper to pick their own and pay what they could afford. A devout Christian who sought the good in others and gave his last to whoever needed it.

His sturdy words to me were "You need to leave here for there is nothing here for you!"

There is a poem in Volume I of "Days Gone By" on page 22 that I penned over 33 years ago entitled "My Father".

He is one of them "A Journey – The Search of the Spirituals."

### Pauline [Minnow] Hopkins - Hickman

My mother was nicked named "Minnow" because she was so small

But! What a talented gifted young girl – a gifted piano player. Upon hearing a piano tune only once, she could play it. Over the years, she became a gifted seamstress, crocheter, quilter, knitter, clothing designer, canning and a fantastic culinarist. Spoke a few words of her mother's ancestors tongue 'Cherokee'.

A strong Christian woman who feared God and guided me to him. Who loved only one man in her 92 years – her husband and my father.

Her words to me "You need to write our history." As she penned to me the relocation of her grandmother and grandfather [Paul Culepper] from Jonesboro Louisiana to Gavalvaston, Texas.

A poem was penned for her in Volume I of "Days Gone By" on page 19 over 34 years ago entitled "My Mother."

She is one of them "A Journey – The Search for the Spirituals"